Summary of

The Road to Unfreedom
Timothy Snyder

Conversation Starters

By BookHabits

Please Note: This is an unofficial Conversation Starters guide. If you have not yet read the original work, you can purchase the original book here.

Copyright © 2018 by BookHabits. All Rights Reserved. First Published in the United States of America 2018

We hope you enjoy this complementary guide from BookHabits. Our mission is to aid readers and reading groups with quality, thought provoking material to in the discovery and discussions on some of today's favorite books.

Disclaimer / Terms of Use: This guide is unofficial and unauthorized. It is not authorized, approved, licensed, or endorsed by the original book's author or publisher and any of their licensees or affiliates. Product names, logos, brands, and other trademarks featured or referred to within this publication are the property of their respective trademark holders and are not affiliated with BookHabits. The publisher and author make no representations or warranties with respect to the accuracy or completeness of these contents and disclaim all warranties such as warranties of fitness for a particular purpose.

No part of this publication may be reproduced or retransmitted, electronic or mechanical, without the written permission of the publisher.

Bonus Downloads
*Get Free Books with **Any Purchase** of* Conversation Starters!

Every purchase comes with a FREE download!

Add spice to any conversation
Never run out of things to say
Spend time with those you love

Get it Now

or Click Here.

Scan Your Phone

Tips for Using Conversation Starters:

EVERY GOOD BOOK CONTAINS A WORLD FAR DEEPER THAN the surface of its pages. Questions herein are designed to bring us beneath the surface of the page and invite us into the world that lives on. These questions can be used to:

- Foster a deeper understanding of the book
- Promote an atmosphere of discussion for groups
- Assist in the study of the book, either individually or corporately
- Explore unseen realms of the book as never seen before

Table of Contents

Introducing *The Road to Unfreedom* 6

Discussion Questions 13

Introducing the Author 34

Fireside Questions 40

Quiz Questions 51

Quiz Answers 64

Ways to Continue Your Reading 65

Introducing *The Road to Unfreedom*

The Road to Unfreedom: Russia, Europe, America, a book written by Yale professor Timothy Snyder, looks at the history of Europe, Russia, Ukraine and the United States to shed light on present political developments that have alarming consequences. The author attempts to uncover myths that veil current political situations in these countries, and traces the interconnections that influence these political events.

The author documents the history of Russian President Vladimir Putin's moves to strengthen his hold on Russia, the invasion of Ukraine by Russia, and Russia's involvement in aiding an American presidential candidate. He elaborates on the two influential beliefs-- the "politics of inevitability" and "politics of eternity." History shows that both are paths that have led to the current social inequality, economic hardships, and the crisis of democracy that nations are experiencing now. The politics of inevitability refers to the idea that progress is inevitable; but economic inequality in the US has shown that this is not true.

The politics of eternity refers to the idea that the past disasters and sufferings will keep coming back to hound people; the government can not do anything about this. Snyder says Putin is using the politics of eternity to hold Russians subservient. Putin subscribes to the philosophy of fascist thinker Ivan Ilyin. Ilyin lived in Europe in the 1920's through mid1950's. He was expelled from Russia for his political beliefs. Living in Germany and Switzerland for the rest of his life, he favored Hitler and Mussolini, creating his version of Russian fascism. Following the ideas of politics of eternity, Putin suppressed historical facts to keep Russians from seeing that they are not as free and better off than people in other countries. Putin rules with the oligarchy, where only a few have access to the country's wealth while the rest of the population have to put up with the poorly run government services. Snyder warns that the social, economic, and political repression in Russia could happen in the US and Europe. Events in the past decade have seen Russia's interference -- Russia's invasion of Ukraine, Putin's denunciation of the European Union, the Brexit referendum, and the election of Trump. The success of the EU and America undermine Russia's politics of eternity. It is the reason why Russia has influenced American and European events to its favor. Snyder believes that though it all looks grim, people can still do something to prevent the worst from happening.

The book is written with a philosophical and historical framework. Snyder says the book aims to understand the interconnected events in history in order to enlighten the present. The importance of historical facts and events is cited, at this time when truth is being questioned. He cites the early Greek historian Thucydides who used historical accounts to clarify the present, and says this book follows his approach. Each chapter thus focuses on a particular event that marks a significant turn in contemporary history-- totalitarian thought and it's resurface in 2011, democracy's collapse in Russia in 2012, Russia's declared disapproval of the EU in 2013, the Ukraine revolution and invasion in 2014, political fiction and its rise 2015; and Donald Trump's election in 2016. Snyder's research included traveling to these areas concerned, and employing the languages of Russian, French, German, English, Polish, and Ukrainian. He compares his understanding of events as a historian to that of the experiences of the people he encountered. The chapters' titles are framed as choices between the values that could uphold or demolish the democratic life: Individualism or Totalitarianism; Succession or Failure; Integration or Empire; Novelty or Eternity; Truth or Lies; and Equality or Oligarchy. Snyder uses clear language, well-researched, and well-reasoned arguments to support his claims. He uses a personal story in his prologue, citing the birth of his son, and the plane crash death of Polish leaders, as signs of a grim future. A comparatively short book, there is force and energy in his writing. He is direct and uncompromising about his views on Putin and

Russia. The theme of the importance of political virtues that show through the facts of history is highlighted, the virtues being individuality, endurance, cooperation, novelty, honesty, and justice. Snyder stresses that these virtues are not mere platitudes but actual forces in history.

Snyder is the author of the best-selling *On Tyranny: Twenty Lessons From the Twentieth Century.*

Discussion Questions

"Get Ready to Enter a New World"

Tip: Begin with questions dealing with broader issues to ensure ample time for quality discussions. Read through all discussion questions before engaging.

~~~

question 1

The Road to Unfreedom: Russia, Europe, America, looks at the history of Europe, Russia, Ukraine and the United States to shed light on present political developments that have alarming consequences. What political developments link these countries together?

~~~

question 2

The author attempts to uncover myths that veil current political situations in these countries. What myths does the author cite?

~~~

~~~

question 3

The politics of inevitability refers to the idea that progress is inevitable. How has this manifested in America and Europe?

~~~

~~~

question 4

The politics of eternity refers to the idea that the past disasters and sufferings will keep coming back to hound people. Who subscribes to this idea? How has it manifested in Russia?

~~~

~~~

question 5

Putin subscribes to the philosophy of fascist thinker, Ivan Ilyin. What does Ilyin propound in his teachings?

~~~

~~~

question 6

Snyder warns that the social, economic, and political repression in Russia could happen in the US and Europe. What political developments point to this foresight?

~~~

~~~

question 7

The Brexit referendum and the election of Trump happened with Russia's influence. Why does Russia want to influence these developments to its favor?

~~~

~~~

question 8

The book is written with a philosophical and historical framework. How does this affect the credibility of the author's claims?

~~~

question 9

Snyder says the book aims to understand the interconnected events in history in order to enlighten the present. Why is looking back to history a good way to understand current events?

question 10

Each chapter thus focuses on a particular event that marks a significant turn in contemporary history. What political events are cited in the chapters?

question 11

The chapters' titles are framed as choices between the values that could uphold or demolish the democratic life. What effect do the titles make on your understanding the book?

~~~

question 12

Snyder's research included traveling, comparison of experiences, and use of different languages. How did these contribute to the book's credibility?

~~~

question 13

Snyder uses clear language, well-researched, and well-reasoned arguments to support his claims. Do these elements help to explain his arguments? Why? Why not?

~~~

question 14

He uses a personal story in his prologue, citing the birth of his son, and the plane crash death of Polish leaders. How does his personal account influence you as a reader?

~~~

question 15

A comparatively short book, there is force and energy in his writing. How does the energy and force show?

~~~

question 16

Yuval Noah Harari, author of the forward-thinking *Sapiens,* says Snyder's book is a required reading for those who want to be illuminated on the current political crisis affecting the world. Would you recommend this book to your friends and family? Why? Why not?

~~~

question 17

The Economist says the book combines reports, history of ideas, and political-philosophical musings--things needed to process facts and ideologies in a roller-coaster world. How do you feel about the rigorous thinking required to process facts and ideologies like what Snyder does? Why is it important?

~~~

~~~

question 18

The Chicago Tribune review says the book carefully documents Putin's power consolidation in Russia and his meddling into other countries' political events. What have you learned about Putin and Russia in this book? How do you feel about Putin?

~~~

~~~

question 19

The Financial Times says Snyder is clear-eyed about American society's weaknesses that invited Russian political interventions. What made America susceptible to Russian meddling?

~~~

~~~

question 20

The Guardian says the book is "chilling and unignorable." What makes it chilling? What can you do to prevent Snyder's gloomy political prediction?

~~~

Introducing the Author

Timothy Snyder teaches history at Yale University. He has published award-winning books Including *Bloodlands: Europe Between Hitler and Stalin* published in 2010, which won the Emerson Prize in the Humanities, and 11 other awards like the Literature Award from the American Academy of Arts and Letters. *Bloodlands*, a bestseller in six countries and translated into over 30 languages, is cited by scholars as the most important book to have been written in this decade. His book *Black Earth: The Holocaust as History and*

Warning was published in 2015 with 21 foreign editions.

Snyder started writing *The Road to Unfreedom* five years ago and was ready to publish it in 2016 but the unforeseen happened: Trump won as American president. He deferred publication and added the part where ideas that originated in Russia had influenced political developments if the Ukraine, Europe and the US. Instead of *The Road to Unfreedom,* he first published *On Tyranny: Twenty Lessons From the Twentieth Century* which became a bestseller.

Snyder highlights six political virtues in *The Road to Unfreedom* namely individuality, endurance, cooperation, novelty, honesty and justice. Calling these virtues as facts of history, he says these are integral to the institutions that uphold such virtues. He says it is helpful to read history because it helps one see the lies being told in the present. History gives a view of the possibilities of the future. This decade is crucial according to Snyder because things can potentially lead to one path or the other. He wants people to see how history unfolds in the present and realize that we have the power to change the course of things.

He says Putin is using the politics of eternity in Russia and Trump is likewise employing the same. His slogan "America First" reflects the idea that there is no future that shows the possibility of a better life but there is a past that was better. This is why the he gives the slogan "make America great again." Snyder asserts that economic inequality in the US has caused politics of inevitability to flounder. It has caused people to question the idea of progress which politics of inevitability propounds. People start to see that capitalism and democracy have not resulted to better lives, and they cannot see a better future anymore. They have become vulnerable to the politics of eternity in the form of Mr. Trump.

Snyder speaks five European languages and reads 10 other related languages. His 10 years in Europe has resulted to several critically acclaimed books, aside from *Bloodlands*, *On Tyranny*, and *Road to Unfreedom.* These books which have translations in other languages include: *The Red Prince: The Secret Lives of a Habsburg Archduke* (2008); *Sketches from a Secret War: A Polish Artist's Mission to Liberate Soviet Ukraine* (2005); *The Reconstruction of Nations: Poland, Ukraine, Lithuania, Belarus, 1569-1999* (2003); and *Nationalism, Marxism, and Modern Central Europe: A Biography of Kazimierz Kelles-Krauz* (1998, 2016). He earned his doctoral degree from Oxford University and held fellowships in Warsaw, Vienna, and Paris. He also held a Harvard Academy Scholarship.

Bonus Downloads
*Get Free Books with **Any Purchase** of* Conversation Starters!

Every purchase comes with a FREE download!

Add spice to any conversation
Never run out of things to say
Spend time with those you love

Get it Now

or Click Here.

Scan Your Phone

Fireside Questions

"What would you do?"

Tip: These questions can be a fun exercise as it spurs creativity among the readers by allowing alternate scene endings and "if this was you" questions.

~~~

question 21

Snyder's book *Bloodlands: Europe Between Hitler and Stalin* published in 2010, won the Emerson Prize in the Humanities, and 11 other awards like the Literature Award from the American Academy of Arts and Letters. Why do you think it won so many awards?

~~~

question 22

Snyder started writing *The Road to Unfreedom* five years ago and was ready to publish it in 2016 but he deferred publication. Why?

question 23

Instead of *The Road to Unfreedom*, he first published *On Tyranny: Twenty Lessons From the Twentieth Century* which became a bestseller. Why do you think it became a bestseller? Do you think he was he right in publishing *On Tyranny* before *The Road to Unfreedom*?

~~~

~ ~ ~

question 24

He says it is helpful to read history. Why? How does reading history enlighten you?

~ ~ ~

~~~

question 25

He says Putin is using the politics of eternity in Russia and Trump is likewise employing the same. In what way?

~~~

question 26

The book is written with a philosophical and historical framework. If Snyder wrote in less academic language and in a popular manner instead, how would it change the book? Do you think it is possible to write it in a more popular language targeting a mass audience?

~~~

question 27

The chapters' titles are framed as choices between the values that could uphold or demolish the democratic life: Individualism or Totalitarianism; Succession or Failure; Integration or Empire; Novelty or Eternity; Truth or Lies; and Equality or Oligarchy. If you are given the choice to write alternative titles, how would you do it?

~~~

~~~

question 28

.It is a comparatively short book. If he made it longer, what topics would you recommend to be included?

~~~

question 29

Snyder started writing *The Road to Unfreedom* five years ago and was ready to publish it in 2016 but the unforeseen happened: Trump won as American president. He deferred publication. If Trump did not win, how would it have changed the book?

~~~

question 30

Snyder speaks five European languages and reads 10 other related languages. His 10 years in Europe has resulted to several critically acclaimed books. If he stuck to English and did not learn other languages, how would it have affected his career as academic and writer?

Quiz Questions

"Ready to Announce the Winners?"

Tip: Create a leaderboard and track scores to see who gets the most correct answers. Winners required. Prizes optional.

~~~

quiz question 1

The author documents the history of Russian President _____'s moves to strengthen his hold on Russia, the invasion of Ukraine by Russia, and Russia's involvement in aiding an American presidential candidate.

~~~

quiz question 2

The politics of _____ refers to the idea that progress is inevitable; but economic inequality in the US has shown that this is not true.

~~~

quiz question 3

Putin subscribes to the philosophy of fascist thinker _____.

~~~

~~~

quiz question 4

True or False: Putin rules with the oligarchy, where only a few have access to the country's wealth.

~~~

~~~

quiz question 5

True or False: Snyder believes that though it all looks grim, people can still do something to prevent the worst from happening.

~~~

~~~

quiz question 6

True or False: He cites the early Greek historian Thucydides who used historical accounts to clarify the present, and says his book follows Thucydides' approach.

~~~

~~~

quiz question 7

True or False: Putin is using the politics of inevitability to hold Russians subservient.

~~~

~~~

quiz question 8

Timothy Snyder teaches history at_____ University.

~~~

~~~

quiz question 9

Snyder highlights six political _____ in *The Road to Unfreedom* namely individuality, endurance, cooperation, novelty, honesty and justice.

~~~

quiz question 10

True or False: He wants people to see how history unfolds in the present and realize that we do not have the power to change the course of things.

~~~

quiz question 11

True or False: Trump's slogan "America First" reflects the idea that there is no future that shows the possibility of a better life but there is a past that was better.

~~~

~~~

quiz question 12

True or False: Snyder is the author of the best-selling *On Tyranny: Twenty Lessons From the Twentieth Century.*

~~~

Quiz Answers

1. Vladimir Putin
2. inevitability
3. Ivan Ilyn
4. True
5. True
6. True
7. False
8. Yale
9. virtues
10. False
11. True
12. True

Ways to Continue Your Reading

EVERY month, our team runs through a wide selection of books to pick the best titles for readers and reading groups, and promotes these titles to our thousands of readers – sometimes with free downloads, sale dates, and additional brochures.

Click here to sign up for these benefits.

If you have not yet read the original work or would like to read it again, you can purchase the original book here.

Bonus Downloads
*Get Free Books with **Any Purchase** of Conversation Starters!*

Every purchase comes with a FREE download!

*Add spice to any conversation
Never run out of things to say
Spend time with those you love*

Get it Now

or Click Here.

Scan Your Phone

On the Next Page...

If you found this book helpful to your discussions and rate it a 4 or 5, please write us a review on the next page.

Any length would be fine but we'd appreciate hearing you more! We'd be very encouraged.

Till next time,

BookHabits

"Loving Books is Actually a Habit"

Lightning Source UK Ltd.
Milton Keynes UK
UKHW041551191118
332602UK00001B/144/P